T0158486

RESTLESS
LIVES

RESTLESS LIVES

poems

HARISH BHAT

EBURY
PRESS

An imprint of Penguin Random House

EBURY PRESS

USA | Canada | UK | Ireland | Australia
New Zealand | India | South Africa | China | Singapore

Ebury Press is part of the Penguin Random House group of companies
whose addresses can be found at global.penguinrandomhouse.com

Published by Penguin Random House India Pvt. Ltd
4th Floor, Capital Tower 1, MG Road,
Gurugram 122 002, Haryana, India

First published in Ebury Press by Penguin Random House India 2023

ISBN 9780143464655

Typeset in RequiemText by Manipal Digital Systems, Manipal
Printed at Thomson Press India Ltd, New Delhi

www.penguin.co.in

To my Muse,
who has taken many seductive forms
over the first sixty years of my life.
I pray that she lives within me forever.

Contents

Preface

Restlessness, catharsis and poetry

I have led multiple lives—some public and others private, some bright and others dark, some that I am proud of and others that cause me shame. There is one binding thread that runs through all these lives – restlessness. My mind tosses and turns for hours at a stretch, refusing to rest.

Throughout all these restless lives, poetry has helped me express thoughts whose existence I had not even sensed earlier. Thoughts that suddenly peek out of their hidden corners when I attempt to express them in verse. Poetry comes closest to an intimate conversation with myself.

Yes, I do speak to myself, which I think is a nice thing to do sometimes, because how else can we pause to hear the depths within ourselves? My poetry attempts to capture these conversations, whenever I can. Sometimes I succeed, and sometimes, the elusive thought just dances away.

That's the thing about many of these thoughts. They have such a fleeting life span, but if caught, they are breathtakingly beautiful, almost ethereal. That is why, when poetry occurs to me, I write it down immediately, even if it is raw.

Maybe it is the rawness that appeals to me. Just as a piece of raw mango can bite into one's tongue, these raw words can bite deep into one's soul, creating a catharsis.

And perhaps that is the whole point of the poetry I write—to create moments of catharsis, counterpoints to the restlessness of life. When brought together, they forge a harmony that is intensely alive.

I hope you discover your own catharsis in these poems born of restlessness. I hope this leads to harmony (of some kind) for you too.

Harish Bhat

A Dog at the Burning Ghats

Long and lazy hours have come upon us
In these winding, untidy lanes
Where cows and pigs live uneasily
On caked and crumbling earth.
Down the road, the fires devour
And mongrel dogs wander around growling
Filthy yet seeking the joy of bitches
In the shadows of the valley of death.

That's not my kind of death, my friend.
It happens all the time around here
I just warm myself by these smoky fires
And forage in these black and ashen mounds
I have learnt not to bark at dead men
Who worship me, the consort of death.
That's it, though. It's not my world though it is
In a different sort of way.

Would it be any different on a warm hearth
Living in the midst of walking corpses
Peering into the secret messiness of absurd lives
While in a gilded cage?
The only true grief is here
The only true journey begins from here
The only true fires are lit at this spot
So it is of course the only truth I know.

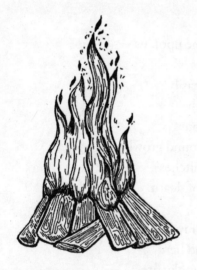

A Single Strand of Fire

My heart has fashioned love tonight
A single strand of fire
The world is throbbing, full and bright
And music storms the lyre.
A wondrous mood, a splendid sight
That a million souls inspire.

A single thread is all it takes
To weave this dream on earth
To cross these misty, sparkling lakes
These forests of our birth
And see our soul which joyous breaks
And sets free from its hearth.

An Untouched Land

Stars are born to rule the skies
Bright and far from fireflies
Untouched, pristine, everyday sought
Every known yet unknown spot.
Immortal burns the untouched heart
Always pining, always apart.

Waves are restless manes that dance
So far from where the chalice stands
The same yet new in every way
Formless, endless every day.
So beautiful stays the unheld hand
A passion, dream, a promised land.

A Summer's Day

A summer's day now once again
A burning, sunny day
Far away from cold and rain
Here sunshine holds its sway

Far beyond the farthest vale
Snow may cloak the peaks
The seas may see a stormy gale
That lasts for hours and weeks

In distant lands, a burst of fall
A splash of colourful sky
A rustling palm, a wailing call
As desert winters sigh

Yet here the sun is fiery hot
A scorching ball of flame
Not a wisp and not a dot
And not a scent of shame

The wilting leaves a'going home
The roots are parched again
Not a soul to wander, roam
And not a lake to drain

Where have the glorious seasons gone
This barren piece of earth?
Will e'er again a springtime morn
Or winter take its birth?

A shrunken face, a distant hope
A silent prayer tonight
May I serve and may I cope
And may I strive to fight.

For burning, scorching sun above
Can never touch my heart
And happy spring of tender love
Can n'er this soul depart!

Caves of Wonder

Silence reigns in caves of wonder
A stillness born of awe
Not a pindrop, neither thunder
Features what I saw.

Crowns and spheres of solid gold
And gems of every hue
Jewels too bright to close behold
And drops of diamond dew.

Lustrous crystals full of light
And million specks of fire
Choicest silver, sparkling bright
A magic flute and lyre.

Within, beyond was endless space
Rushing still so calm
Its darkness bound in distant rays
Now cold and yet so warm.

Rainbows, moons and starry streams
Lit this splendid sky
In its vastness floated joyous dreams
Growing wings to fly.

But not a whisper, not a sound
Is heard or seen in sight
Silent reigns the sacred ground
Cloaked in wondrous light.

Priceless riches seek no face
Need no tongues to speak
Their brilliant, dazzling, winsome rays
Win every heart they seek.

Endless Journeys

Dying has no end and living has no end
The road to nowhere never has to bend
There is no heart but only a soul
There is no end but only a goal
A star that we sight but once a while
The distance, my friend, is always a mile.

Why do you yearn so soon for my earth
Your womb is no cell but a beautiful birth
For often you dream and perchance you dance
Sometimes a smile and sometimes a glance
A journey we walk now clutching a hand
Across these transient mounds of sand.

Who?

Who goes in quest of fire tonight
For warmth or touch of light?
Who roams the forests, black in white
In pursuit of your sight?
The skies don't flicker, the stars don't shine
The fire's just not bright.

Who dreams these castles high on land
On rock, on ice, on desert sand?
Proud and strong they roar and stand
Mighty, haughty, strong and grand
But not the laughter, not the dance
These are not the dreams on hand.

Who sleeps this joyous bed of peace
In calm, in storm, in fragrant breeze?

Goodbye

Goodbye and farewell, my little baby girl
May angels carry you far.
May heavens their flags with triumph unfurl
As you near the evening star.

Goodbye from afar, for thus was life
Paths that seldom dared to meet.
Never a tear, and never a strife
Yet never a day so sweet.

Goodbye my lovely, silent maid
Did you hear the thunder roll?
It made me wonder, a little afraid
For the milestone and the goal.

Goodbye tonight, and adieu for long
Look down, watch us, now and then.
Sometimes take us all along
And sometimes wish us fond amen.

My Little Haunted House

I thought I saw a small little spider
Run on an edge which just got wider
A bumblebee stopped and turned around
Why should I fly so far overground?
It was strange that the rest of the crumbling house
Had not a single cat or mouse.
Is it mildly haunted, this room gone dark?
Are the ghosts gone out for a walk in the park?

A fish climbed in and asked for a drink
There was none at the bar, orange or pink
Yet it was strange the rest of the town
Was waiting to see the strawberry crown.
It's foolish, said the man, there's no work here
I wish I just had a cold mug of beer.
These ghosts who are gone ate all my food
And then they drilled large holes in my wood
But it is strange we shut down the place
Why should this house just fall from the race?

Haunted house come and haunted house dance
Spider and dragonfly rise from your trance.
Switch on those psychedelic blinking lights
Kick off your boots, run up those heights
When it's strange that floors just drop and drop
Then images scream and images stop.

A monkey smiled softly in my dream last night
And my little haunted house just fell from sight.

Hope on a Sunday Morning

A parrot is within this park each Sunday morning,
Red and canary yellow with a rising joy.

Green feathers stick out in bright anticipation
A brown little beak holds a tasty little worm
It swoops down upon me, and then flies away.

In such a moment lies much of our universe
A small little, happy little, bright little dream
That slips out when the heavens open, just a little ajar
Unseen by an unsparing wooden world
And so my parrot is my muse.

You may well be a fugitive from paradise
Yet you are a prisoner of hope
Sometimes a distant flicker of flame
And elsewhere a blinding roar of light.

Every day. Every day my parrot is my own
For though it never comes home, and always flies away,
It will always, always be back in my park
Each anxious, cheerful Sunday morning.

How Vibrant Runs
This Splash of Earth

How vibrant runs this splash of earth
How colourful flows the sea
What beautiful canvases take their birth
To astonish you and me!

So bright, so stark, so much surprise
At this delicious feast
They spark the mind, delight the eyes
These gorgeous, fabulous beasts!

All around, in every heart
Their colourful parade's on
Some come in, and some depart
Each brilliant twilight morn.

I've roamed the earth, in constant quest
Of magic, love and joy

Yet here and now I take my rest
My senses to enjoy.

For I've never seen so greatly bless'd
This garden once exiled
For I've never seen so richly dressed
So bright these dreams, so wild.

Glimpse of Paradise

Will I ever find a glimpse of paradise
Silent, soft and flowery pink
Tossed in golden sands and waves of nectar
Washing up on this empty shore?

Forbidden to turn my eyes so skyward
The moon and stars seek refuge within
Darkness marks no antidote to light
Not ever in Eden, and not tonight.

And the fire keeps burning, burning, burning
Devouring a little bit here and there
Turning its tongues to small little whispers
Unknown dreams and wastelands fair.

Will I ever chase my end of the rainbow
With a smile and a free and a happy heart?
In colours that smile and splash so brightly
Or will I just be here until I depart?

Lost in Tranquility

Our cocoons are scattered across the world
Often curled up, or unfurled
Until we drop into their gaze
Softly, unseen, warm embrace
Moments that dive into our mind
Or prise it gently from behind
Despite the hunger, march and din
We suddenly voyage far within.

Oh, we suddenly voyage across seas
On shafts of light or flights of geese
Beautiful emptiness all around
A silent compass, mind unbound
Sometimes a prison, sometimes a door
Sometimes a shadow over the floor
Are these the twilight zones of day
That amble in and swoop away?

Oh, we amble in and out of pace
In a freeze that binds both time and space
Pinhole heavens of such delight
You soften hearts and widen sight
You make us wonder, night and day
In a light and passing sort of way
Where do we go, and why do we scream
When all we can do is smile and dream?

Oh, when all we are is all we are
When all we seek is a silent star
Amidst comets, rainbows, moon and shine
In this enchanting world that's only ours
In languid thoughts of here and now
Quiet moments that fall from above
When Kings and Queens and you and me
Are lost in tranquility.

Madness

Eighty-five years of starlit stillness
Where silence echoes clearer than sound
And the madness expands into swirling space.

Like a terrible sweet and raging voyage
That knows no end tonight,
That knows no end other nights now either
Pulsing, racing, floating, gloating
Not a form and not a gesture
Not a thief yet not my Lord
But a million dreams that fight.

Have you seen these stars, my lonely friend?
Have you watched the moon glide by,
Wearing the robes our King has gifted
As he drifts past in the sky
Silence, watch that distant, flickering point of light.

And then the galloping pounding thunder
Chariots full of royal blood
Hooves that run and rush by panting
Glorious joyous mind-blowing happiness
That knows no end tonight.

Moments of Madness

Our moments of madness
Burst open with joyous violence
A great and sparse peace spreads out
As that needle swims away
Carrying just the tiniest spot of blood.

We own them yet we disown them
Once or twice we even clone them
But it's never ever the same
Like so many golden drops of honey
And so many flying sheets of flame.

The heavens also dance with abandon
Blanketed by the dark and serene sky
The stars, the only pulse of passion
Sometimes to shine, sometimes to cry
Maybe to shout, but always to die.

Our moments of madness
Are ours to cherish and celebrate and hide
In secret songs of boundless happiness
Which whisper to us some moments we pave
Until they become our endless tidal wave.

My Stalker Takes a Million Forms

Murmuring streets
Stalk me tonight.
Silent swirling vapours
And distant unseen light.
Forlorn are the swamps
Desolate the sight.

Greetings at this gate my friend
There never was a key
Kindly leave your Gollum out
At least pretend to be free.
We have a welcome drink for you
And you can choose to be.

Wrought iron gates
Are shut as they speak
Mock me like a paradise
That's turned arid bleak

I will wait and turn away
Search yet never seek.

The Emperor sends you greetings
And this stone so lustrous bright
We'll do a little painless check
To make sure you're all right
Then we have a house of gold
Where you can rest from flight.

Rooms of shining silver-gold
Prisons of my days
Mirroring those dreary marshes
Of indifferent haze
My stalker takes a million forms
But will never change his ways.

Of Bankers and Billionaires

Said the banker to his billionaire friend
Let's talk of many things.
Fat bonuses and Ponzi schemes
And bailouts fit for kings.
Why bother with dud PE funds
Until the fat lady sings?

Why bother with silly interest rates
When they're bound to drop much more?
With all this time on our clean little hands
Let's shop for a Greek marble floor
Or a Picasso that's up for sale tonight
This old landscape's such a bore.

Obama's capped our pay, I'm told
But our bank's dining cards are here.
So let's fly our jet to LA tonight
And do a meal so sheer

Caviar and truffles are just the thing
To accompany Belgian beer.

Did you hear that global growth is down
And may go all the way to nil?
And the pound is diving like a stone
Against stubborn British will?
Our carmakers on the verge of a fall
But wait, would you like a refill?

Here's the first sub-prime paper I sold
See how bright and clear it reads
What promises it held out day and night
The saviour of so many needs
Such a pity it's been ruined by
These small homeowners' greeds.

Perhaps you'd care for some oysters now
This place serves them salty-cold
I meant to tell you all this time
I keep forgetting, I'm getting so old
Do you recall the large stock portfolio
You advised us to hold?

Worth a cool six hundred million
Largest we've held, my love.
Our chief trader's run it to the ground
It's worthless as of now.
Would you like another drink perhaps
Before I take my bow?

On Seeing a Bright and Brilliant Morning Star

A silent, dark and tranquil pool
Assumes exuberant form at dawn
Its waters like a mighty ocean
Around this brilliant spot
This epicenter of the light of life
This single, sparkling, luminous star
More magnificent in its glorious contrast
Than a million suns today.

This is its triumph of calm
A lone spot of genius that seeks to light,
And shine, and dance, and dazzle—
Yet never intrude or overwhelm
The restful dawn.
This is indeed its lesson of love
To celebrate, and to guide,
And to embrace in its luminous arms
A world now free to choose.

The sun may be the essential source of life
The morning star yields a richer harvest
The timeless, precious gift of love.

Quiet Inspiration

The loudest inspiration is very quiet
It speaks through actions
That reveal thoughts
Which create words
That live on in history.

It quietly composes pulsating new music
That sets the dance floor rocking
The only conversation
The rush of liberation
And the magic of the dance.

But behind these heady beats
The new composition remains
A brave and lonely voyage
Of a mind that is determined
To mercilessly tear open new skies.

Quiet inspiration moves our world
Shapes our deepest dreams
Hurls a million vials of energy
It is the purest form of adrenalin
Known to mankind.

Music of Your Dance

May the music of your lingering dance
Be soulful, vibrant, slow and pulsating, all at once.
May the shimmering mosaic of this dance floor
Come alive in a thousand colours and contrasting hues
In the unending folds of a raga that lifts away the timeless
A song that wafts through the desert with an unstoppable
    haunting energy
A ferocity which is as beautiful as the soft caresses
Of a life that believes in life.

Of a life that believes that creation has so many forms
So many rhythms, so many wide-eyed moments of awe
Of a life that explores ceaselessly, and dances with abandon
Always restless, always wanting one last dance,
    and one more then,
Before the evening melts away.

May this dance go beyond its night and dawn
With an energy that refreshes every limb and soul

May the music play on, and all its various notes
Continue to create and recreate the magic
Of a marvellous life.

Reflections on Clouds Seen from the Window of an Aircraft

Are these clouds but a mattress of the sky
Soft as our snow and so incredibly high?
Where are the Gods, on their glorious steeds
Do they cross by these skies, and stop by these reeds?
Is the sun, though so strong and so hot
Cut off by such peace, where no battles are fought?
Are these clouds so pure, a testament of love
Of the Goddess below, and the heavens above?

But wait.

Are these darkening spirits, so restless and so loud
Purveyors of hate or carriers of shroud?
Why should they be so grey, so brooding and dark
When the parched earth's happy and flowers in the park?

First looks can deceive but can never take away
The happiness of love and the waters that stay.
When do they live, these clouds of the sky
Do they live when they live, or live when they die?

The World Has Finally Stopped

I heard the world has finally stopped.
And I wonder why.

Is it something we did
Or some secret we hid
Or that gooey sticky stream of blood
That ruined our backyard last week?
Such a rapidly spinning thing
No forewarning, not a ring
And now it's stopped. Like my darling little watch.
Like my blingy thingy watch with diamonds in it
Now hard and frozen, no light to shine
Oh, that's because the lights have also gone
Searching for the missing dawn
I wonder why.

Is it something we never spoke about
Some lingering, packed up, shameful doubt
Like those shredded limbs we suddenly saw

On our beautiful lawns last week?
Questions for you, questions for me
Questions that'll never let us be
People in a world that's finally stopped
Where we lived too long for free.

Shadows of Space

Shadows of space
Clinging to these walls
In tenacious silence
Formless listless vacant shapes
Endowed with a stubborn life
And a creeping crawling goose-step search
For a non-existent soul

Insipid endless passages extend
Beyond these parasites of time
Neither past nor future beckons
And the present struggles within
A silent intractable death
Every single day

Wailing in their stillness
Like some mute banshees
Multiplying in their loneliness
Like a million friendless amoeba

They suck out every oasis
Arid dusty barren lifeless
A great unquenched thirst
That kills and kills and kills

Dark shadows of space
Gloomy obstinate tentacles
That shrink and shrivel life
Go away
Go, before I die again.

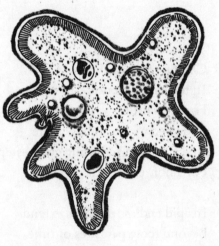

Shadows Swim in Shallow Waters

Shadows swim in shallow waters
Unknown beasts that surface like black submarines
Which have dropped ballast abruptly
For very little reason, often none at all.

Great celebrations often occur in absolute secret
In the dark of life's most shameful moments
But what is shame, and what is glory?
And why should I ever chisel my story?

Rainbows always disappear without trace
Though sometimes the Cheshire Cat smile remains
Mocking, haunting every barren moment
Of the abyss we have left behind.

Still As Rain

The stillness of this rain
Rides its torrential deluge
A sheet of frosted glass
Set against furious skies
An inexplicable tranquility
That disowns itself
Time after time after time.

On these wild and misty moors
A hermit threads the beads of time
Silent in his great agitation
Like the vast and soundless cosmos
Hurtling past its margins.
The stillness of this rain
Time after time after time.

The Glorious Colours of Spring

I feel so young, I feel so high
I feel a oneness with the sky
I feel so bright, I feel so alive
I feel this urge to fly!

See colours break, see colours swim
See colours dance to light
See sparks of spring on heaven's rim
See magical worlds so bright!

I smell my flowers both red and green
I smell the silvery dew
I smell grey smoky fire that's been
O smell the sky so blue!

I sense the colourful fluttering wings
I sense a rainbow smile
I sense the lord of colour and rings
Has been here all this while!

The Morning Star

A single bright and fiery star
A single spot of light
So sharp its rays and yet so far
Oh, what a wondrous sight!

The sky is silent and so dark
The world is fast asleep
Not a single movement in the park
When to my eyes you leap

A beam of brilliant silver light
Magic in your breast
A stream so soothing in its sight
This dreamy midnight quest

Come and charm us every dawn
Come speak in tranquil voice
Till you blend or flee the morn
So peaceful in your poise

Morning star, come light my dreams
And shine into my eyes
Softly, softly, yield your streams
Till the twilight sighs.

The Mountains

These craggy peaks have grazed the sky
Since its dreamy days of birth
As far back as time can fly
Always deep and always high
Always testing worth.

Set against the hazy blue
Their earthy stone
Marks a contrast sharply true
So stark it breathes in every hue
In every life and tone.

On skies they dance our distant hopes
These crests a lofty height
Strong with rough but sturdy ropes
Sometimes steep and slippery slopes
But always clear to sight.

They set a pursuit great and long
Sharp to view and breach
Always firm and always strong
Unlike skies which make you long
And stretch beyond your reach.

These craggy peaks are here to stay
As you fondly skyward gaze today.

I Need but Just a Song

Who cry today they grieve for life
For no freedom marks this heart
They drift apart, they mourn this strife
Till death does make them part.

A thousand deaths, each day on day
A million tiny shreds apart
Once a colourful canvas may
Turn a shroud and far depart.

Catch these smiles so far and few
Hold them tight tonight.
Catch these buds with twinkling dew
Tears that burst with light.

Who dream today they thirst for wine
Purple, rich and strong
Unknown lands, full of sunshine
And perhaps just a song.

Shallow Excesses of Satiated Men

the shallow excesses of satiated men
cast a long and pallid omen
smirking in their hedonist caves
safe, secret, brooding raves
empty touch, recurring urge
life now exults its own dirge.

a winter's night is close at hand
a storm that lashes mounds of sand
a head that longs and craves and aches
and hunts for shiny frozen flakes

do they forget the heart they own
seeking peace, yet all alone?

an army stalks the empty skies
a one-night stand now barren dies
but hordes of mammon rush to fill

staring voids and endless till
these the empty fires they know
nowhere do these waters flow.

To a Schoolgirl
Who Ended Her Life

A twisted mind drove you to leap
From a cliff that knew no end
Now you will forever sleep
You could have lived, my friend.

What thick clouds of dark and grey
Kept the sunshine from your life?
What made you see the night in day
What struggles and what strife?

Sometimes we exist, seen but unseen
Objects of pity and helpless eyes
Why me, my God, why have I been
Hung by my own fears and lies?

Where does death end its empty call
And where does liberation begin?

Why does life end in such a fall
What is the quest, and where is the sin?

Farewell little girl, angel of some dreams
We did not deserve your soul.
The world will carry on, mindless it seems
Having made its unjust toll.

Tonight the Fires Burn

Many many fires burn here night after night
Many many leaves fly
Many many dreams slip out of sight
Often a tear, and often a sigh.

The breeze is so sparkling, so calm and so free
It drifts like the moon on a silent night sky
Is this dark smile but a smirk on a tree
Is this the way to learn to just die?

Or is this the train of a rudderless thought
The columns of smoke which exist no more?
A hunt for a treasure so avidly sought
Yet neither the sea, and never the shore.

Many many hearts have broken on this rock
Many many souls have lingered and fled
These are the keys, and this is the lock
This is my life instead.

Immediately upon Reading *The Inheritance of Loss*

(A tale so poignant, so human and so likely to be true, that reading it is a catharsis I never really knew)

You sold me a thought
You bought me a dream
You fed my little lot
Icy waters of a stream.

You invaded my door
You carved out a cave
I hungered for more
For my heart was your slave.

I laughed and I flew
I danced and I cried
Very quietly I grew
As I sat by your side.

Thanks for a world
With pieces that I know
In your womb I was curled
As I ebbed in the flow.

How beautiful the tale
And how soft is the tear
For each time that we fail
Only love do we fear.

For each time that we rise
Only love is at hand
Sometimes in a guise
But somewhere on my land.

The Sky in Your Head

Don't carry the sky bobbing in your head
It has stars you will never find
Though black holes long since gone and dead
Will always eat your mind.

Strains of music, wine and love
That have long since flown away
Grey beneath, and blue above
The remnants of a day.

Don't catch the rainbow, it's such a cheat
It always floats away
It's always apart, and never complete
For more than half a day.

Tarry awhile, and watch the sky
As it spreads and makes to fly
You may long, and you may sigh
You may watch it by and by
Yet it'll never belong, who knows why.

Musings on Love and Life

Who grieve tonight they grieve for love
Who laugh they laugh for life
Who dream tonight they think of how
They walk through peace and strife.

Who talk tonight they talk of love
Who sing they sing to dance
No seeds, no fields to till and plough
Stark the bareness stands.

Who fly tonight they fly for love
Who soar for freedom soar
The eagle always kills the dove
Yet they always look for more.

A Den at Nightfall

It is dusk and the time when a haze does spread
All over the sky and around your head
There is a sadness that hangs out of nowhere
And stays for a while, before it departs
To wherever it came from, nowhere.
It's all in the clouds, which are pregnant with rain
Yet so fearful of precipitation tonight
There is this fear that hangs out of nowhere
And then it cries, and it cries, and goes away
To wherever it came from, nowhere.
When the sun goes down, come sit right here
Smell the haze, and whistle at the clouds
Feel these cheeks, hollowed by the years
Take a deep breath, no sadness or fears
Yes, they are gone, for now, nowhere.

A Song of Siachen

(Written as a tribute to the soldiers who have died while defending distant Himalayan glacier)

Frozen wasteland, coffins of snow
Why do we fight, and where will we go?
Will ice ever melt in this bitter cold
For the mountain is young, but man grows old.
Listen, gently, to that orphaned cry
Louder than these gusty winds up high.
And then sit down, to polish and spit
Raise the flag, and dig the pit.
All at once. So long, and yet so soon
There will come this wonderful moon.
A nice bright sky for the dance of death
With mighty guns and frozen breath.
Stop my friends, halt this now
In name of God and timeless love.
These hills are meant for dreams and awe
Not for crushing hearts and claw.

Make a snowman, dress him with white
White for peace, and respite.
White for mourning, for these young men
Who perished so lonely, on Siachen.

Musings on a Broken Tooth

Yesterday a large tooth tumbled from my mouth
Broken, aged, chipped and tired, it suddenly slipped south.
I mourned for just a moment, thinking of all the fun
Munching, biting, slurping, sucking, all there and done.
Fifty summers, trusted friend, hardy molar on my gum
Used you for everything, aloo dum or rum.
Never thanked you, never paused, to think of all the grind
When you fell, only then did you enter in my mind.

Then with my tongue I felt the hole that you had left behind
Sharp and jagged, dark and hollow, a cavity most unkind.
Your broken edges cut me sharp, time and time again
Sometimes very numb I felt, and sometimes sharp in pain.
But then I heard you say to me, why mourn me just now
You had all these years, big mouth, to show me some love.
Now that I'm done and gone, you'll face the dentist's blues
What you take for granted, is always yours to lose.

Colours of Tears, Colours of Hope

This time the colours, they run through my tears
It is filled with sadness, this worst of our years
A procession of deaths, of solitude and loss
Colours of smoke, and loneliness that was
This time the colours, they are lovelorn
Waiting for you, to be reborn.

This time the colours, they hold out our hope
They tell us softly, to get out of our mope
They splatter and they dance, with an unseen smile
A song from the heavens, after all this while
This time the colours, they want us to be strong
We'll soon be back, and it won't be long.

Just Read Me Your Song

Don't play me your music
Just read me your song
Standing by the culvert
So narrow and so long
There's so much in this party
But maybe not for me
Dancing down the river
Then drowning in the sea
Who is live and who is dead
Who shall ever know
Except he who dives within
And he who wants to go
So wake up now and say your piece
Take your songsheet out
Let your words flow like the breeze
Stirring us and flowing out.

Grabit Man

Hey man, walking in, for a little bit of rain
A little bit of sunshine, and a little bit of Spain?

This and that and everything, all you want to be
Snatch it now, and pick it fast, everything you see.

Grabit man, grab it, you own the sun and earth
You are revered by your halo, and blessed by your birth.

No one to speak to, and not a soul to thank
Jimmy old boy, you've reached such a rank.

Grabit all the time, for that's the fashion now
No questions ever asked, and not a hint of love.

Holes in the Wall at Jallianwala Bagh

So empty are these holes today
Yet so full of dusty silt.
Is stone so prone to sleep and fray
And deaths to silent wilt?

Look below, bullets are strewn
They are one with lifeless sand.
You are I are not immune
But neither will we stand.

Some night, fresh blood will flow
From these holes in the fraying wall.
When bodies leave their graves and glow
Be ready, my friend, for the fall.

These bullet holes, they hold our blood
Our nation's wounds and pride.

We salute those who faced that flood
Whose determined faces kissed the mud
Whose courage changed the tide.

Jallianwala Bagh, a hundred years now
You remind us starkly, of our deepest love
Always our nation, above what is mine
This is our reflection at your shrine.
This is our prayer, and this is our vow.

Don't Search for Answers

They never tell us the answers, do they
Always questions, always more questions
And the silence of the grandfather clock
That has unwound its own day.

They may not know, after all
The ignorant rule the parched earth
Deluded into staring at the skies
Which have no answers to provide.

For tonight, just for the night, you can fly
In a stupor, you can dream
Of answers that will never be yours
Colours that will never fill this empty canvas
Because your time hasn't come. Not yet.
So don't ask. Don't speak. You are not expected to.
Turn on the music, and let the numbness flow
A time to turn down, or just a time to go.

Parting and Death

Parting leaves an invisible residue
In the thinning glass of life
Always forward, and always too few
Friend, concubine or wife.

Death is better at playing this game
The glass just chips away
So without a wisp of teary shame
You can go all numb and grey.

I Know You Will Sing Tonight

I know you will sing tonight
At a place so far away
Out of reach and out of sight
But I will hear you say
What you have said a million times
Holding back your tears
Simple words and pleasing rhymes
That suppress your own fears.

Now you've woken up and flown
To such rapturous applause
Do you still recall the stone
That we would silently toss
Into the waters where your song
Would burst so fresh and free
Inviting us to dance along
And be what we would be?

I know you will sing tonight
Songs of the long lost dove
And in our corner, dimming light
I will listen, my love.

Missing My Heart

I wake up today, in pitch darkness, and stumble around
Missing my heart, numbing my mind, skipping my ground.
When did she go, no whisper, and no note, and no death
Taking her mattress, her mixed smells, and her heavy breath.
We'll meet, on some highway, on a random chance I guess
And then we'll say, hey, where were you, no more and
    no less.

Like strangers we will kiss with hesitation and embrace
Beyond those vibrant nights, and without those silent days.
And then we will race, towards our distant, reddish skies
Once again, we will pass by, towards our very own highs.
This is my bed, my friend, this is the only womb I know
This is where I try to love, and swim, and leap and grow.

I cannot find the candles, but I will walk on in the dark
And sit forlorn, in this beautiful midnight park.
I know the sun will rise no longer, and it will cast no
    single light

It has sneaked off like you, petty thief, totally out of sight.
So let me listen keenly now, to every little sound
It may help me find my heart and mind, somewhere on
   this mound.

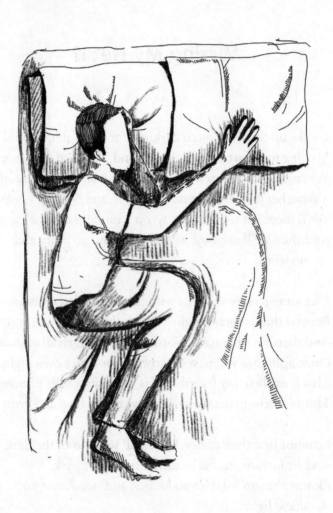

Moods of the Coronavirus—Poetry of the Pandemic

Heart and Mind

We died. We died and we lived a little, and then we
    died again
A deep fear cast its spear into our minds
Casting heavy curtains against the light.
But our heart, our brave and pounding heart
It rushed towards the mind, and tugged at that spear
With ferocious love. With love and hope,
Which have never been beaten. And never will be.
The steel is now gone, the wound may heal with time.
Or it may decay and disease and die.
Heart and mind, the battle is yours to win.

Silence

The silence of life
Haunting, scary
Empty, wilting
Here and now.

The silence of life
Beautiful, nourishing
Peaceful, happy
Here and now.

The silence of death
Belongs to God.
But the silence of life
Belongs to us.

When Shall We Dance Again?

So much time since the music stopped
Tracks too hot to resist.
So many days since the curtains dropped
Oh so many nights since we kissed.

All this emptiness, where will it go
Will it finally drown in the sea?
Without the flight, and without the flow,
Where will our passions be?

So much darkness since that moonlit night
How long will these dark clouds stay?
It doesn't feel good, it's just not right
What we've done to ourselves today.

Perhaps with hope, and prayers that rise
These clouds will vanish with rain.
Clear sweet water, falling on our eyes
And then we'll dance again.

Oh My Mama

One more ping, and one more life
No sign of struggle, war or strife.
Oh my Mama, why did you hide
Why did you trample, upon my pride
When all you had, was to say a word
Or a thought that gently, softly stirred
But here's a ping, and now she's gone
Oh my Mama, why were we born?

One more ping, and there's data to see
Figures to analyse, beyond destiny.
Oh my Mama, what song did you sing
That gave these vultures soaring wing
When all you had, was to wave your wand
And ground them in this slimy pond
But here's a ping, and now we move on
Oh my Mama, why were we born?

One more ping, the last siren goes on
Oh my Mama, why were we born?

Restless Life

Some small and uneven pebbles have rolled
Towards these sparkling waves tonight.
I believe these are spangled thoughts
Of various magnitudes and flashes of gold
Yet can I halt such trickles of flow
With a wave of my desperate, flailing mind?

For when madness rages, there is often peace within
A drifting kind of listless, groveling peace
An endless night sky which swallows its fiery comets
As a whale, and then it glides on.

I see these stones, and I wonder and I wonder
How endless are these zones of distress
How eternal these blue and orange skies . . .

The static peace of death can never really hold a candle
To the rich and rolling peace of life!

Self-Preservation

Who is right and who is wrong
You'll never know, so sing along.
Sing the song that you desire
It may gently ebb the raging fire
Far from heaven, a warmer earth
Until a distant second birth.

These are the courts of a powerful King
Forever now, lord of the ring.
You must be silent, until you speak
Safety lies in being weak
So till the truth be finally told
Be content now with growing old.

When bugles seem so loud and clear
Be on guard and carefully hear.
For the notes that lie, within the sound
For the dusty wind, that flies around

In this palace are many locked doors
You'll never know which, men of the floors.

Get up now, and make your bow
You must be seen, and show your love.

Song of a Rainy World Inhabited by Vultures

The rainbow has melted, and fallen in the sea
So the fish have had to pack up and flee
The vultures are here, with their claws of steel
Cutting through the clouds, and digging in their heels
They fly to soft music, seductive and cool
Struck by a DJ, in a disc for a fool.

A million raindrops are waiting in the hall
No one wants to break out and fall
Yet they will, and the vultures will drink
These drops of red faster than you think
Tonight the bar will have bottles of blood
Neat or stirred or blended with mud.

The clouds look jagged and worn and weak
The head vulture opens its beak to speak
Men and women, give us your hearts

Place them gently, in our shopping carts
We'll sing your praises, loud and clear
Don't cry now, there's no need to fear.

Don't cry now, we want your love
For we are just a larger, stronger dove
Your hearts will be totally safe with us
For ever, and ever, within our truss
The rains are here, let's skip and prance
Let's join you now, in one last dance.

Thank You for
Giving Us Wings of Fire

(A tribute to A.P.J. Abdul Kalam)

You gave our minds great wings of fire
You gave our hearts fine thoughts of gold
You took our sights higher and higher
To a great strong nation, beyond the fold
You urged us, come, walk, inspire
Dream your dreams, big and bold.

These missiles of the mind that you made for us
Where were they forged, and what did they bear?
How did you charm this entire land
With your twinkling smile, and your flowing hair?
You taught us to grow, and yet like a child
How did you lead us to this fantastic fair?

Missile man, missile man, hear us once more
For we rise to the wondrous sounds we heard

We rise to thank you, for paving this path
For reaching our youth, with passions stirred
We the nation, we wish you well
As you fly away, on your beautiful bird.

The Colours Are Gone

The colours are gone.
Just like that. Totally gone.
They only existed within our irises
Which are now faded and jaded
Crouching in search of a new day.
But the sun is still the same, my love
So where will fresh light come from
And how will my new winds blow?

There are memories, of course.
And that's why the mind trumps the eye.
Glorious years of quick young dances
And motorcycle journeys on scorched earth
This is a baton I carried like my own.
Which it never was, my love
We must now consider the sunset
Beautiful, orange, by the ebbing tide.

The earth searches for its youth, once more.
Give it your eyes, and give it your heart.
There is no fountain, but there is a past
And maybe a new sun also, soon
From some black hole, that we've never seen
From some high tide, that has never been
If the past can paint this canvas today
We will live, and smile, and love. Again.

The Pink Sky

The evening sky has turned a beautiful shade of pink
A most bashful colour, that peeps out from a veil.
Stare silently, and look beyond the far-off brink
It's time to sit down now, and then to set sail.

Break the brown bread, and pour the purple wine
This is the hour to listen to your heart;
To the memories that have always been secretly mine
And the moments that try to tug and depart.

You may never see the birds of the pink sky
They hide themselves until the true darkness falls.
They know everything there is, except the why
For example: why the music stops, and why the night calls.

Sometimes, if you want to, you can roll up your mind
You can tie up the loose ends, and stack it all away.
Leave the debris buried, deep and far behind
And fly off to the pink sky, in a reckless sort of way.

These are the moments of magic and of tears
Gaze and feel and touch them, they are all about you.
They eclipse the world, until everything clears
And then the pink sky turns its everyday blue.

Song of a Disturbed Night

I don't want to watch the sea tonight
Its waves are not an easy sight
So should I sleep, or should I roam
The street outside my broken home
Should I dance, or should I sing
Until my mind takes gentle wing
Tell me, tell me, am I right
To seek a little streak of light?

Maybe it is the whispering time
For a haunting piece of nursery rhyme
That does not leave my throbbing head
Fallen, broken, cracked and dead
I see him jumping up and down
An orange yolk in a dressing gown
And then I ask, what should I do
When you have lost your sheen of blue?

Talk to me, you fallen star
Talk to me, you sea so far
Talk for everything and now
Years and years of starlit love
All I need are silent tones
Bit of warmth within my bones
I want to rise, I long to fly
One more time, before I die.

I Counted and I Lived

I counted one million stars last night
And then they shut me down
So the zeroes simply vanished
Do they ever count, really?

But it was fun while it lasted
I got to know a few stars personally
Some black holes as well
And some exploding supernova.

Particularly the constant explosions
The noise was so comforting
It shut out the deafening silence
And helped me live. And count.

Live. And count.
Like a man possessed
Until I heard the distant bell
And just then, the lights went out.

Be My King

Why are you dancing up and down
Are you a king or are you a clown?
Are you so scared of the towering tent
Or the way those earlier jokers went?

Sit down and think what you really are
And why you've come so long and far.
This may require an honest mind
Which I admit isn't easy to find.

Chase these courtiers from your hall
Before they trip and make you fall.
And then in silence turn your way
To think outside gold and grey.

Often sunshine, sometimes night
Hasten joy and carry light.
And then you can always be my King
With a well forged, wise and golden ring.

Each Time

Each time I reached that page, I cried
Though the story was never the same
The tears they welled and came
Because someone somewhere died.

Each time I walked this path, I sang
Like a man so light and free
It was never what I would see
But always that bell that rang.

Each time I rose and called your name
Wary of what I would find
A different picture comes to mind
Though you are still the same.

Each time I rest and sip my tea
I try to exclude strife
Yes, it's a different time in life
But it's the same and same old me.

As I Keep Living

Must I welcome the night
With apprehension and love
Or should I live on in the day
And dance away?
They tell me life rarely
Has a single right answer to offer
They tell me the search
Has to continue until the very end
And so I keep asking without thinking
Keep listening without choosing
Keep moving without dancing
I keep my sanity that way.
So let's keep talking and talking
Around the questions forever.

Dawn, Let Me Sleep

Dawn has crept upon me like a thief
And now it pretends
To be my friend
Because it thinks'
That sunshine has the power
To right all wrongs.

But this is not the case, my friend
Sometimes the sun can burn
Or get eclipsed for a moment
That lasts for all time
With forlorn memories
Of my stolen dreams.

It is best that we embrace
And go back to our sleep.
The daylight will wane
And leave us in peace.
For this thief is a lover
And this lover is a thief.

A Piece of the Sun Came Visiting

A very small piece of the sun
Broke away and lodged itself
In the interstices of my home.
We saw it and we wondered
Whether it would rise and set
Or whether it would sleep
All day long.

Would it warm us softly
Or burn us very hard
Or give us fresh rays
To see things anew?
Would it lose its heat
And die tonight
Or grow and explode
With blinding light?

A few hours later, it left.
We forgot to ask

Why it had come
And how we could help.
We forgot to offer
A cup of tea
And have a small chat.
So all these questions
Will stay with us
And will be discussed forever.
That is the way of our world.

On Coital Confusion

Coital confusion is a terrible thing.
Until it is numbed by sex.
Then too, the dark night stretches
Like infinity that has gone to sleep
Deep within both of us.

This bed is haunted by our hearts.
We so casually left behind.
So there is no calming lamp here
Only a raging leaping fire
And a tiny, tiny speck of light.

Coital confusion is a beautiful thing.
Until it is numbed by sex.
Then the day arrives and we
Step beyond our beds
Into our jaded, elegant lives.

The Pursuit of Loss

The beauty of loss is the loneliness of love
Fleeting moments, just far above
Dusty streets that do not settle
Missing warmth and empty kettle
This is the space we sought, my friend
We lusted for this aching end.

Was there a shimmer of gold out here
That led us blind, bereft of fear
Hoping, dreaming, chasing the wind
Often chaste but sometimes sinned
It did not matter how we ran
This was our goal, we must, we can.

And then we found this garbage heap
After our climb so breathless, steep
Set against the orange sky
What a spot to dance and die
There are the stars, there is the pain
There is the dry and missing rain.

The Safety of Nights

The nights are always safer
They hold you in a dark womb
That cradles all your fears.

Dark nights, come upon me
Numb and starlit, warm and soft
Fast asleep.

Sleep is always safer
But never mind, for tonight
I am here to watch the skies
Darken, darken, and recede.

That too, is just like sleep
Without its eyelids on.

These night skies
They are so beautiful
They are so far away.

This Empty Room

This empty room
It smells of you
Breath and skin
Sweat and dew.

Your kindly eyes
Hold back my tears
They make me calm
And numb my fears.

This empty bed
Where does it go
Will it fall apart
Or its memories grow?

This empty floor
It yearns for you
Its windows ache
This listless view.

I hold the door
Its welcoming hue
You hear my knock
Both old and new.

This empty room
It smells of you
Breath and skin
Sweat and dew.

When the Soul Begins to Speak

When the soul begins to speak it gurgles slowly
Like a stream that is just stirring from its sleep
And then it murmurs words that are yet to form
And songs whose lyrics are lost to my ears
I know it is struggling to connect and narrate
After years of isolation in a golden cage
Passions have taken their abrasive course
And now I feel the call of my age.

And then it awakes like a storm unleashed
Rushing in to make up for all that is lost
My goblet of wine shatters on the floor
Like blood that has boiled and spilt
I sit very still, and listen to this song
Wafting and dancing, strident and long
There is no escape from a woken up soul
So I lift up my eyes, up from my hole.

When the Year Fades a Little

When the year fades a little,
What faces do we see, hiding in that haze
Ruby red reflections, distorted by chipped crystal
Sediments of a lingering sadness
Ambiguous dreams that only pause
To comprehend their own little puzzles.

I am the giver and the receiver of these visions
And their wild and vacuous ghosts
That bicycle, or run, or chase the sun
And sip on rare, organic craft nectars
In a freshly divided world.

When the year fades a little,
Turn up the music, and walk away
Many colours will beckon to you
It's a safe choice to stay with grey.

Where Are We Going?

Where are we going, my friend, my friend
Is this the start, or is this the end?
Where is the fork in the road that we took
Did we dare as we did, or did we not look?

Why do we walk this wrinkled down lane
All this fresh dust, and here's a new stain.
It's going to coat us, now or in time
Why do we walk, amidst this grime?

What are these masks, that surround us now
Ghoulish greyish faces, devoid of love.
Take them away, oh, take them afar
And fly me then to my favourite star.

Farther from here, and everything away
I'm tired, my love, it's the end of my day.
Hope in my heart, but now it needs rest
I don't need hatred, and I don't need this test.

Hold me so tight that my bones crack a bit
And we kiss, and we kiss, and we silent sit.
All by dark waters, this stillborn lake
Once upon a time, it was ours to make.

Where are we going, my friend, my friend
How long can you now this walk extend?
How long before the dark of the sky
Beckons us softly, to sleep, and to die?

Words

Did your words curl up with you in bed
Tired, sobbing and terribly drunk?
Are you ashamed of them, my love
Because they lead such an empty life
Within your throbbing, swollen skull?

You should make them dance again
And again and yet again, until they leap,
And fly away. Because they were never yours really
These severely moulting butterflies
Who want to taste every flower, everywhere.

Someday, maybe some will return
And haunt the corners of your very old thoughts.
Raise them from the beautiful enamelled coffins
Ghosts that laugh madly and sob sadly
Until you join them, in a sort of immortal afterlife.

The End

There is no end
Only a bend.

This last page
Is only a stage

Where this song
Can belong

To your heart
And not depart

Yes, time to mend
But there is no end.

Acknowledgements

This volume of poetry has been possible only because of the encouragement and support I have received from Milee Ashwarya, publisher, Penguin Random House India. Thank you, Milee, for your belief in my books, for constantly nurturing the writer in me, and for now launching me as a poet too.

Dipanjali Chadha, my editor, has not just edited this book, she has shaped it so beautifully from start to finish. Her superb editing skills are only matched by her ability to coordinate seamlessly with multiple stakeholders. I am an unabashed admirer of her craft, and I am grateful for her unstinted partnership in the creation of this volume.

Saloni Mital brought to this book her mastery of the English language. Her meticulous edits ensured that each poem emerged fitter, tighter and cleaner. Thank you, Saloni.

Sanchita Mukherjee has given a very special life to this book through her superb illustrations. She has evoked the emotions of each poem through her visual imagination and art. While doing so, she has also left pleasant space for the reader's own interpretations. Sanchita is a very talented artist, and I am grateful to her for having agreed to illustrate this book.

My wife, Veena, has been my constant partner in all my writing endeavours. Her love and support have sustained my writing voyage over the years. She has been a strong votary of my publishing this book of poetry to mark the sixtieth year of my life. From the poems themselves to the cover image and the illustrations, she has also promptly provided me her candid views which have inevitably helped me with making the right decisions.

Our daughter, Gayatri, loves the written word, and I have greatly valued her observations about some of my previous books. I hope she likes this book when she sees it.

To my mother, Jayanthi, and my mother-in-law, Vatsala. I thank them for their blessings which sustain and nourish me. They are the elders of our family, and their unconditional love and affection make me a better human being and a better writer every day.

My grateful thanks to Goddess Saraswati, for blessing me with the passion, capability and constant urge to write. I hope and pray that I continue to put this wonderful gift to the best possible use throughout my life.

I am amazed that every single acknowledgement above is to a woman. Do you think poetry, in its essence, is feminine?

Scan QR code to access the
Penguin Random House India website